Why Are The T-Rex's Forearms So Small?

Everything about Dinosaurs Animal Book 6 Year Old Children's Animal Books

BABY PROFESSOR

EDUCATION KIDS

In this book, we're going to cover interesting facts about the Tyrannosaurus rex, one of the scariest dinosaurs that ever walked the Earth. So, let's get right to it!

MESOZOIC ERA

These giant dinosaurs lived during the Mesozoic Era during the late Cretaceous Period from 65 million to 70 million years ago, which was the time period right before dinosaurs went extinct. They were one of the last types of big, meat-eating dinosaurs.

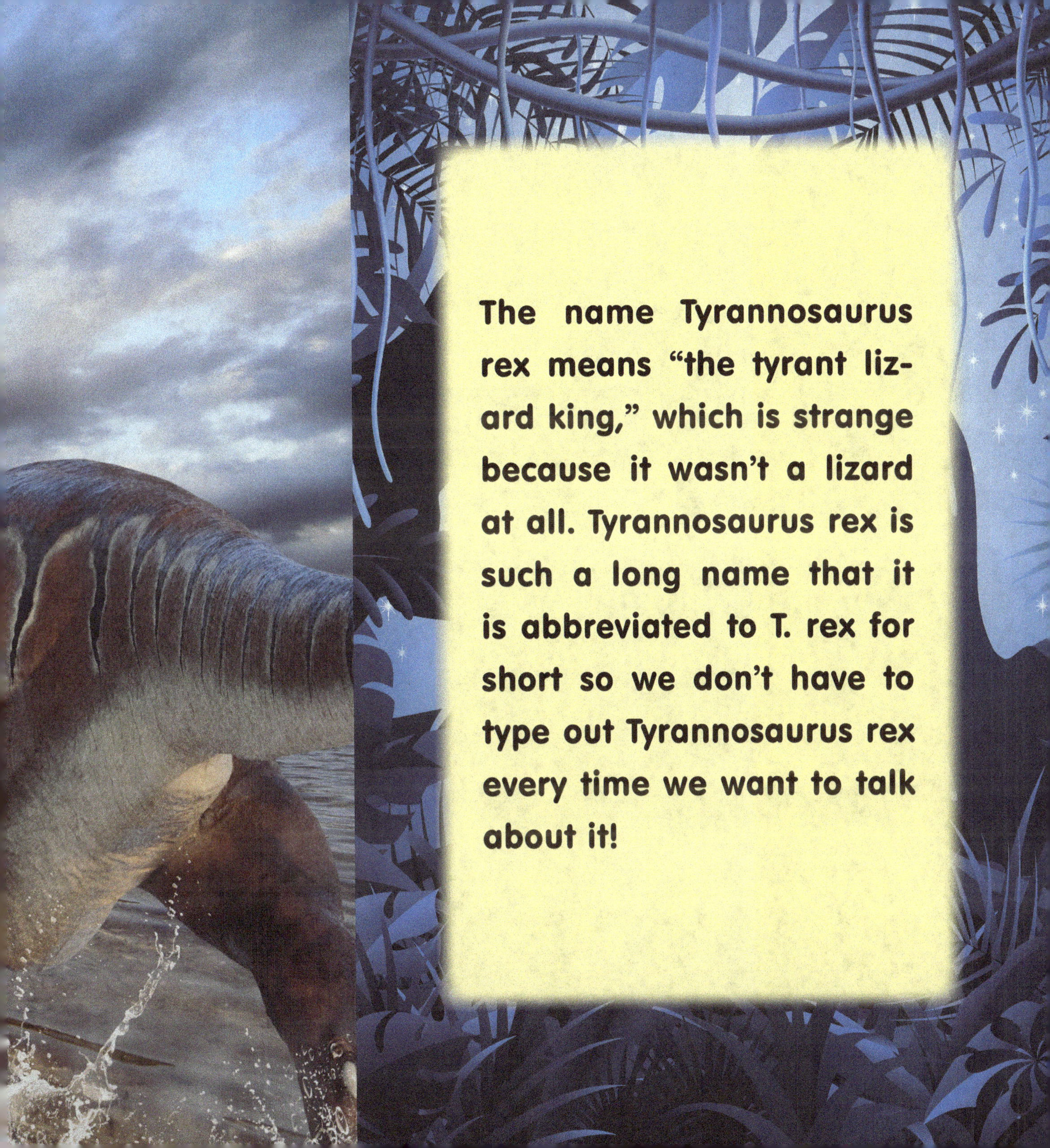

The name Tyrannosaurus rex means "the tyrant lizard king," which is strange because it wasn't a lizard at all. Tyrannosaurus rex is such a long name that it is abbreviated to T. rex for short so we don't have to type out Tyrannosaurus rex every time we want to talk about it!

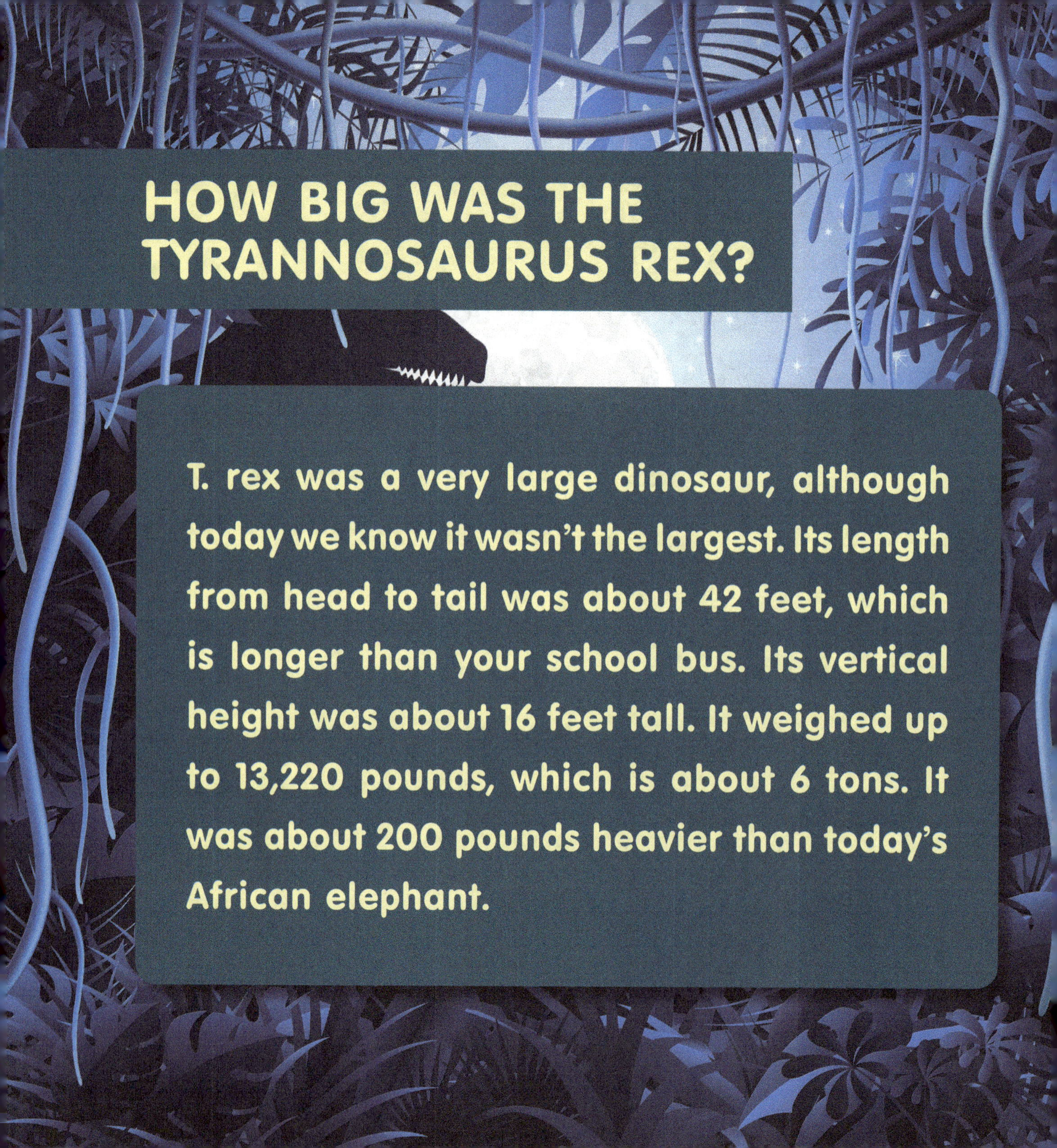

HOW BIG WAS THE TYRANNOSAURUS REX?

T. rex was a very large dinosaur, although today we know it wasn't the largest. Its length from head to tail was about 42 feet, which is longer than your school bus. Its vertical height was about 16 feet tall. It weighed up to 13,220 pounds, which is about 6 tons. It was about 200 pounds heavier than today's African elephant.

Its hind legs were very strong. Each leg ended in a foot with three toes. It looked something like a bird's foot only much, much bigger! It walked on its two hind legs. Its whole body was tilted forward and its body was supported by a long, stiff, strong tail. The tail had as many as 42 bones in it.

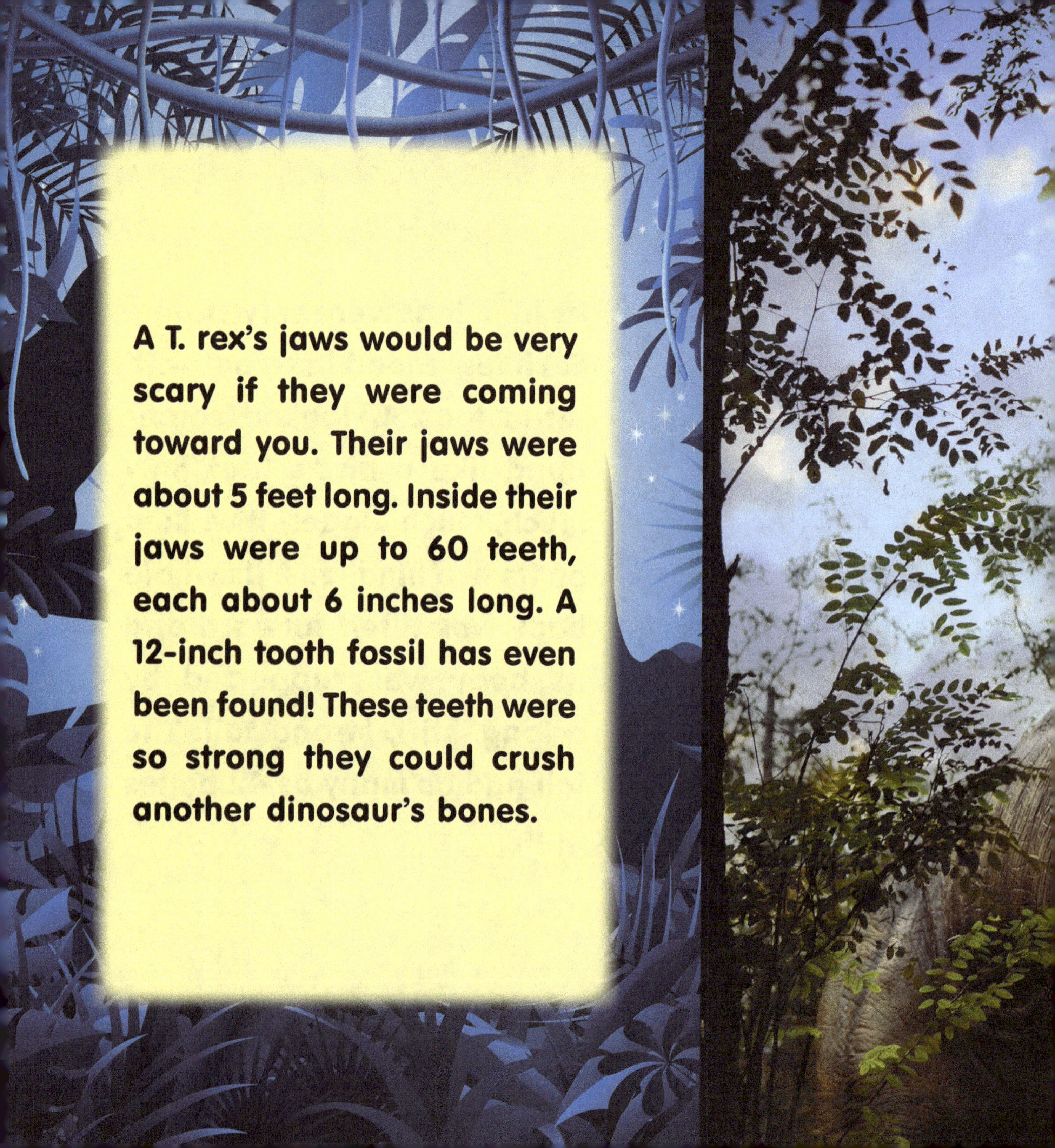

A T. rex's jaws would be very scary if they were coming toward you. Their jaws were about 5 feet long. Inside their jaws were up to 60 teeth, each about 6 inches long. A 12-inch tooth fossil has even been found! These teeth were so strong they could crush another dinosaur's bones.

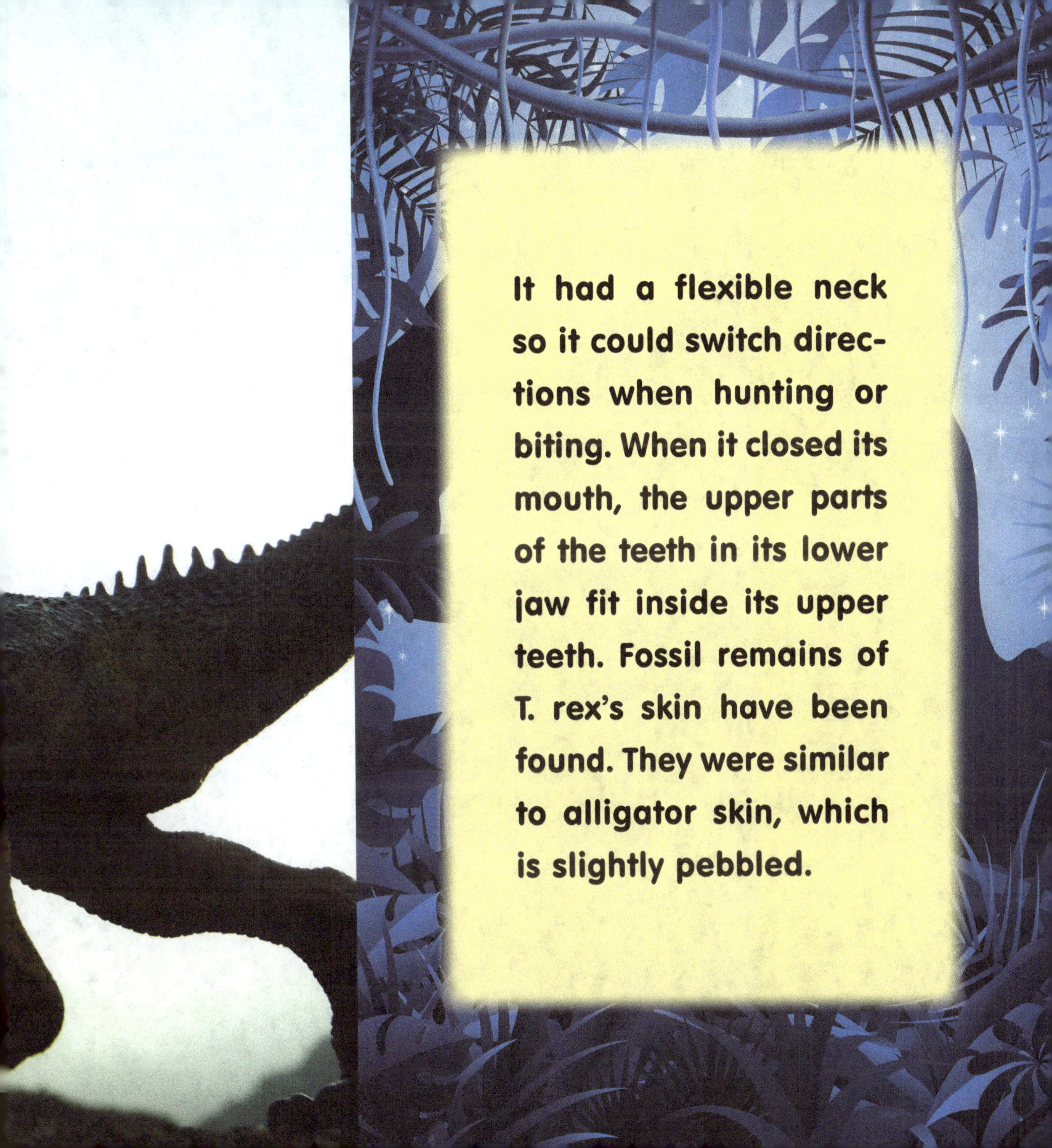

It had a flexible neck so it could switch directions when hunting or biting. When it closed its mouth, the upper parts of the teeth in its lower jaw fit inside its upper teeth. Fossil remains of T. rex's skin have been found. They were similar to alligator skin, which is slightly pebbled.

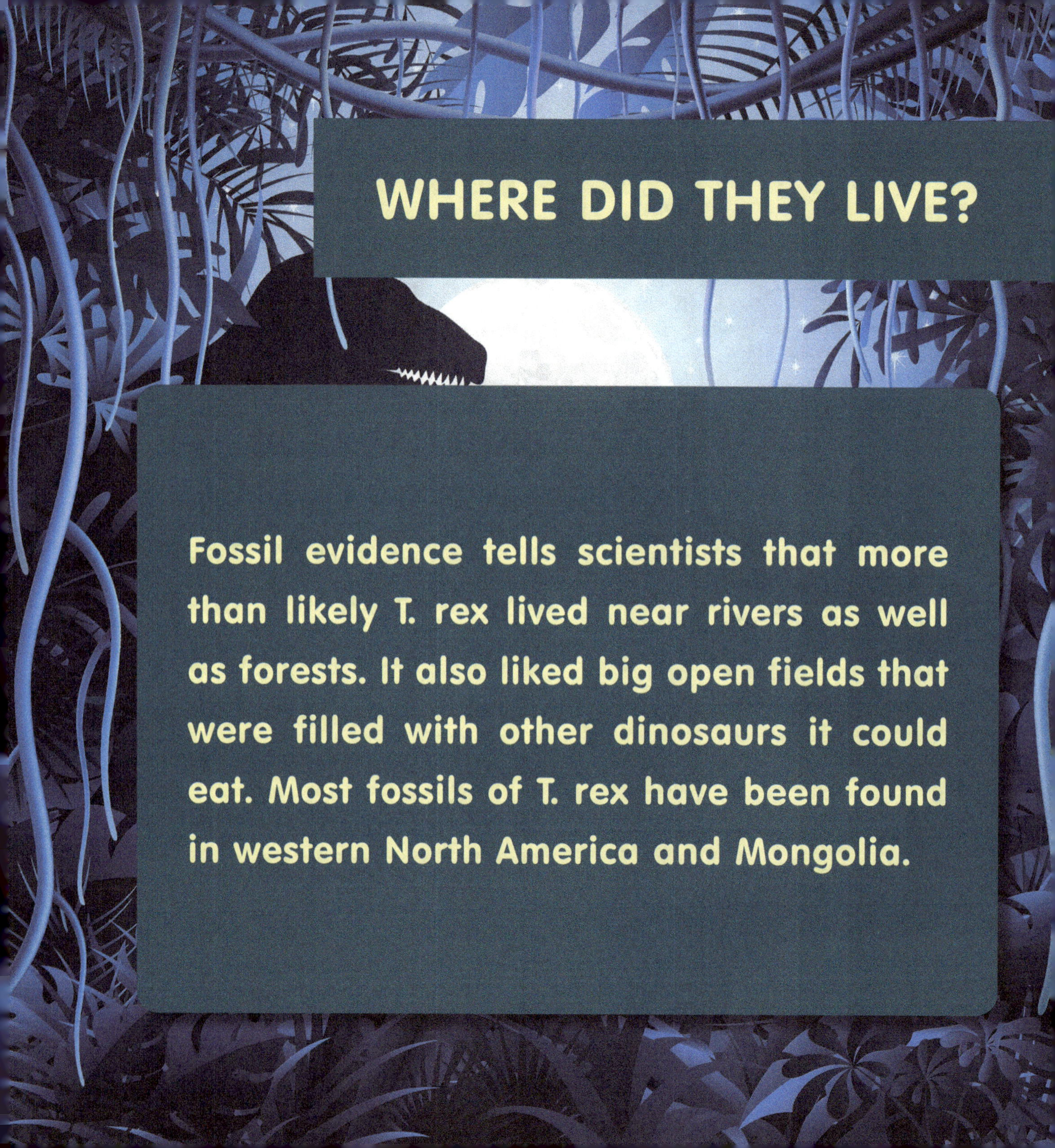

WHERE DID THEY LIVE?

Fossil evidence tells scientists that more than likely T. rex lived near rivers as well as forests. It also liked big open fields that were filled with other dinosaurs it could eat. Most fossils of T. rex have been found in western North America and Mongolia.

HOW DID TYRANNOSAURUS REX WALK?

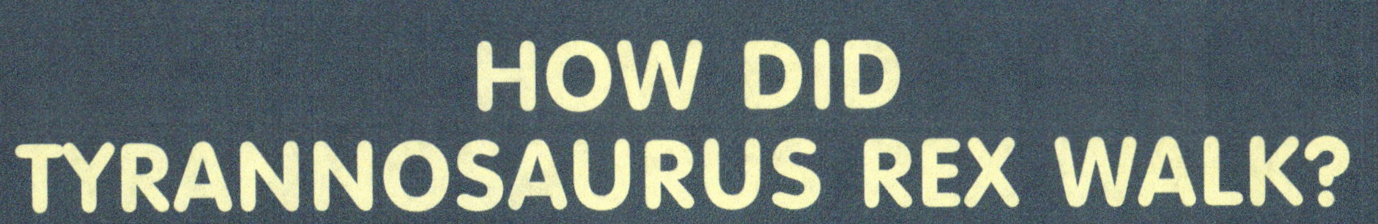

T. rex walked on its two massive hind legs, which means it was bipedal. Scientists are still debating whether its tail was on the ground as it walked or in the air. Recent experiments with birds seem to show that T. rex kept its tail in the air when it walked.

Some scientists put fake tails on chickens to see how they would walk since chickens are direct descendants of the T. rex. If you've ever watched a chicken walk, you would notice that its head is pushed way forward from its body. This is how scientists believe that T. rex walked too.

Chicago
Museum

Barnum Brown

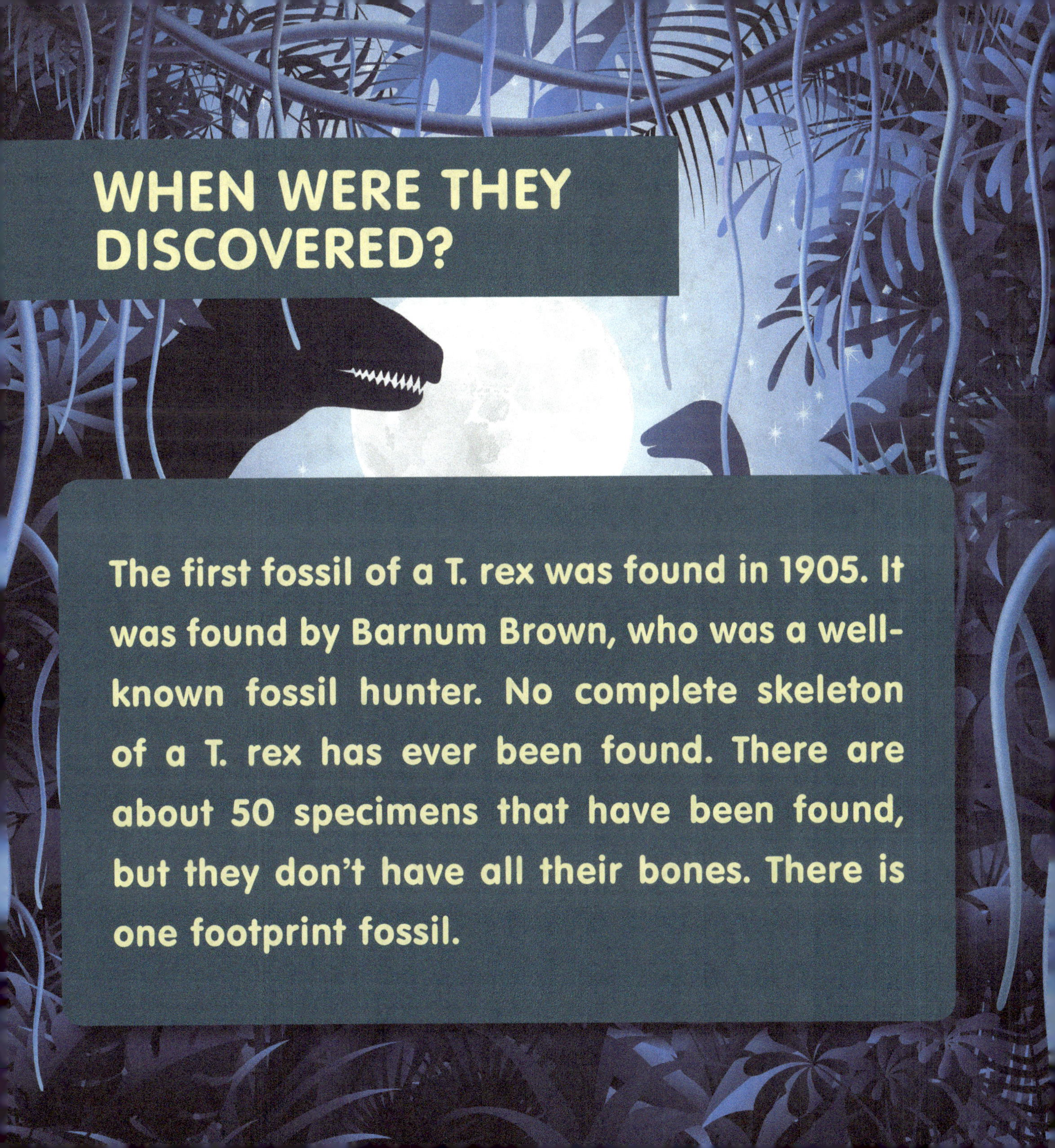

WHEN WERE THEY DISCOVERED?

The first fossil of a T. rex was found in 1905. It was found by Barnum Brown, who was a well-known fossil hunter. No complete skeleton of a T. rex has ever been found. There are about 50 specimens that have been found, but they don't have all their bones. There is one footprint fossil.

WHAT DID TYRANNOSAURUS REX EAT?

Tyrannosaurus rex was a carnivore, which means that the T. rex ate meat and lots of it. Scientists believe it could eat 500 pounds in just one bite. It ate other large dinosaurs such as Edmontosaurus, Triceratops, and Anatosaurus. It could have swallowed small dinosaurs up in one large gulp!

Some scientists think that T. rex was only a scavenger. A scavenger is an animal that only eats dead animals. These scientists think that T. rex wasn't fast enough to track, hunt, and kill its own food. Other scientists believe that this huge dinosaur both hunted on its own as well as took food from other dinosaurs.

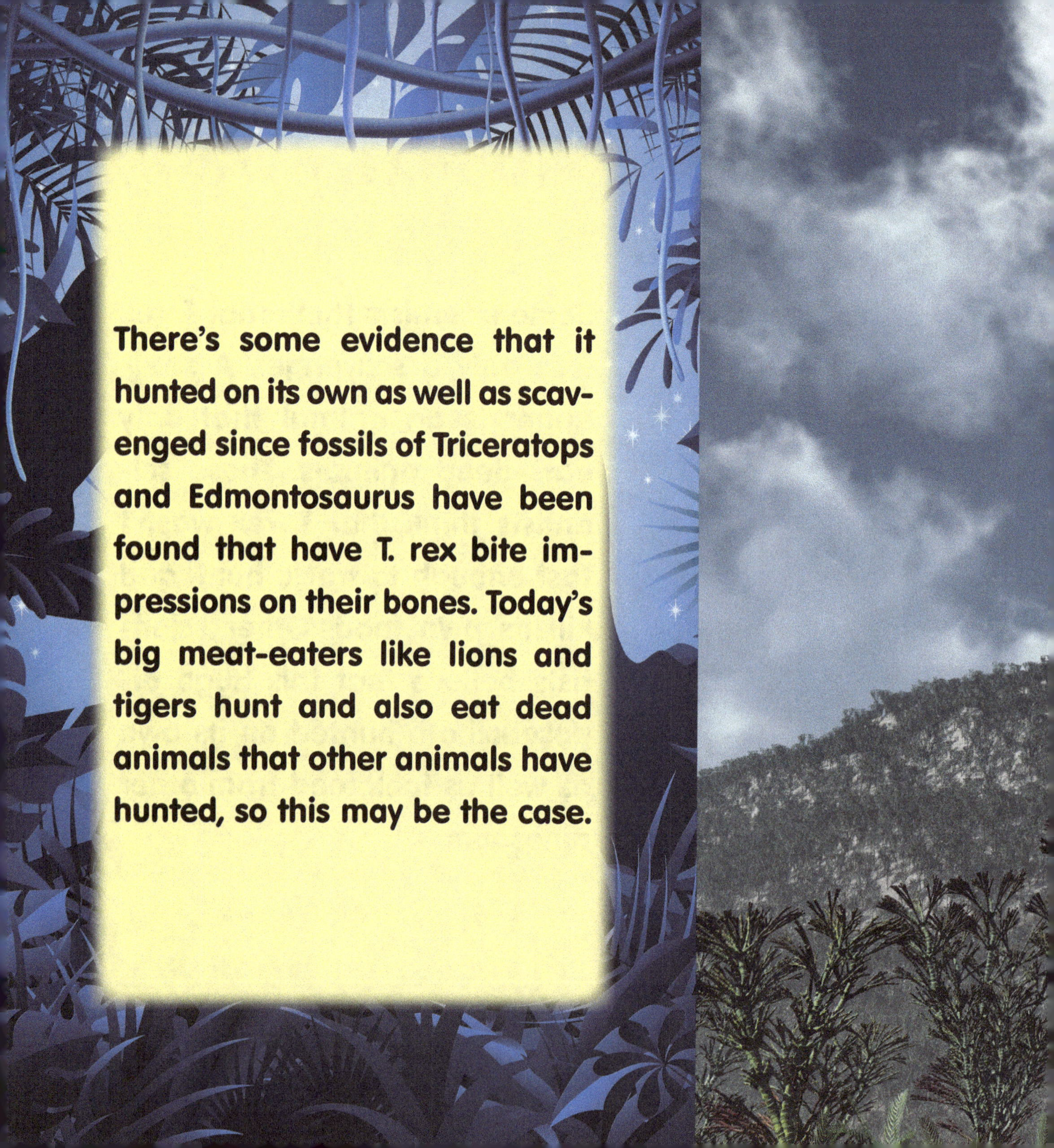

There's some evidence that it hunted on its own as well as scavenged since fossils of Triceratops and Edmontosaurus have been found that have T. rex bite impressions on their bones. Today's big meat-eaters like lions and tigers hunt and also eat dead animals that other animals have hunted, so this may be the case.

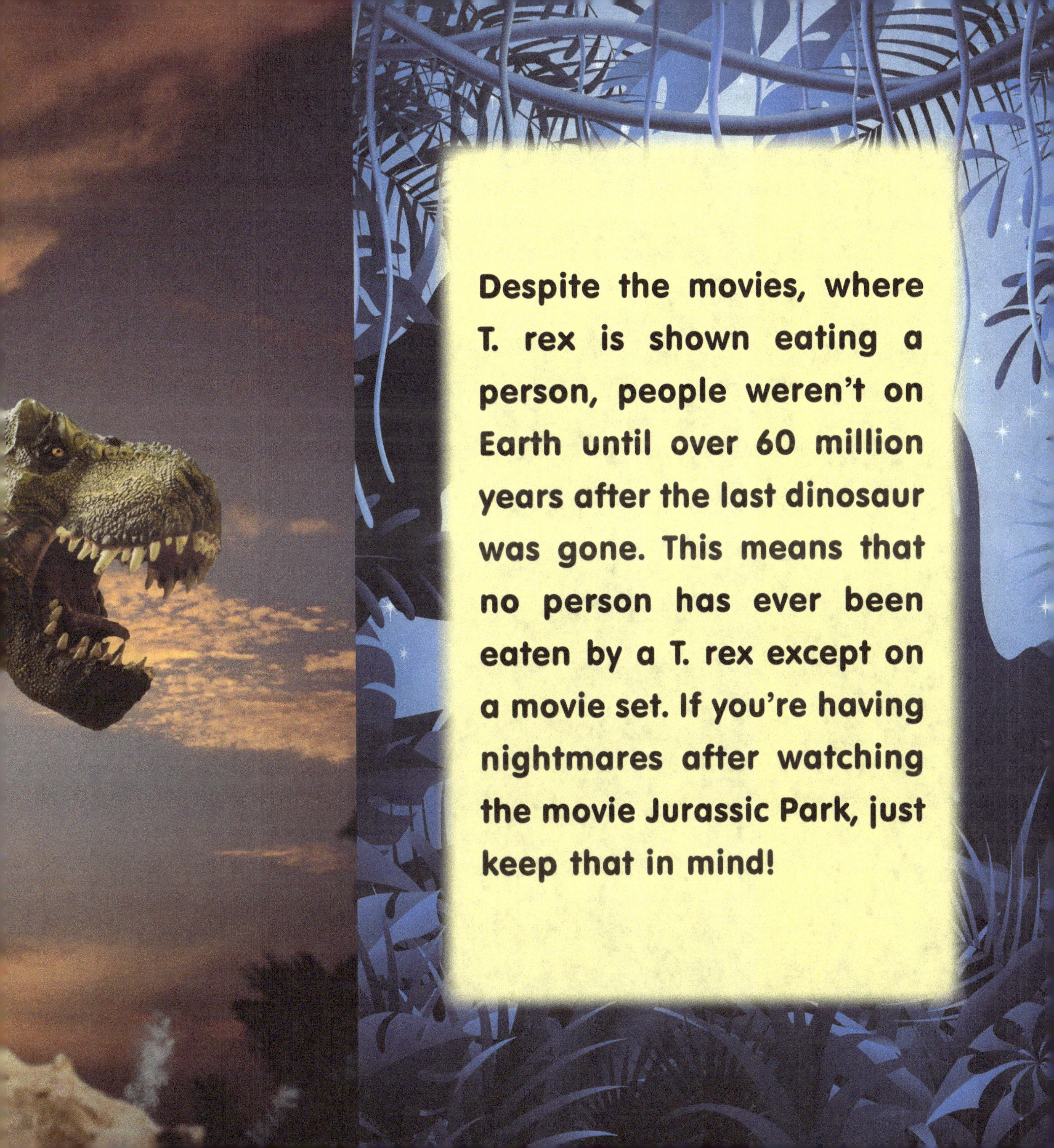

Despite the movies, where T. rex is shown eating a person, people weren't on Earth until over 60 million years after the last dinosaur was gone. This means that no person has ever been eaten by a T. rex except on a movie set. If you're having nightmares after watching the movie Jurassic Park, just keep that in mind!

WHY WERE ITS ARMS SO SHORT?

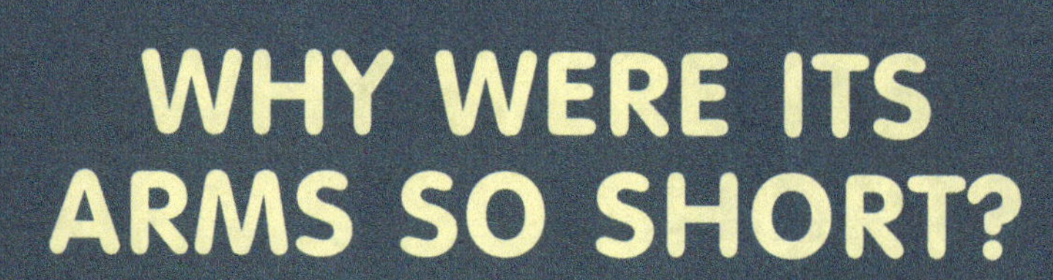

The T. rex was such a big creature, so why were its arms so short and its front claws so tiny? Scientists are not completely sure but they have lots of theories. It couldn't use its arms and claws to put food into its mouth like we can, because its arms were too short to get all the way up to its mouth. It couldn't touch one arm to the other either.

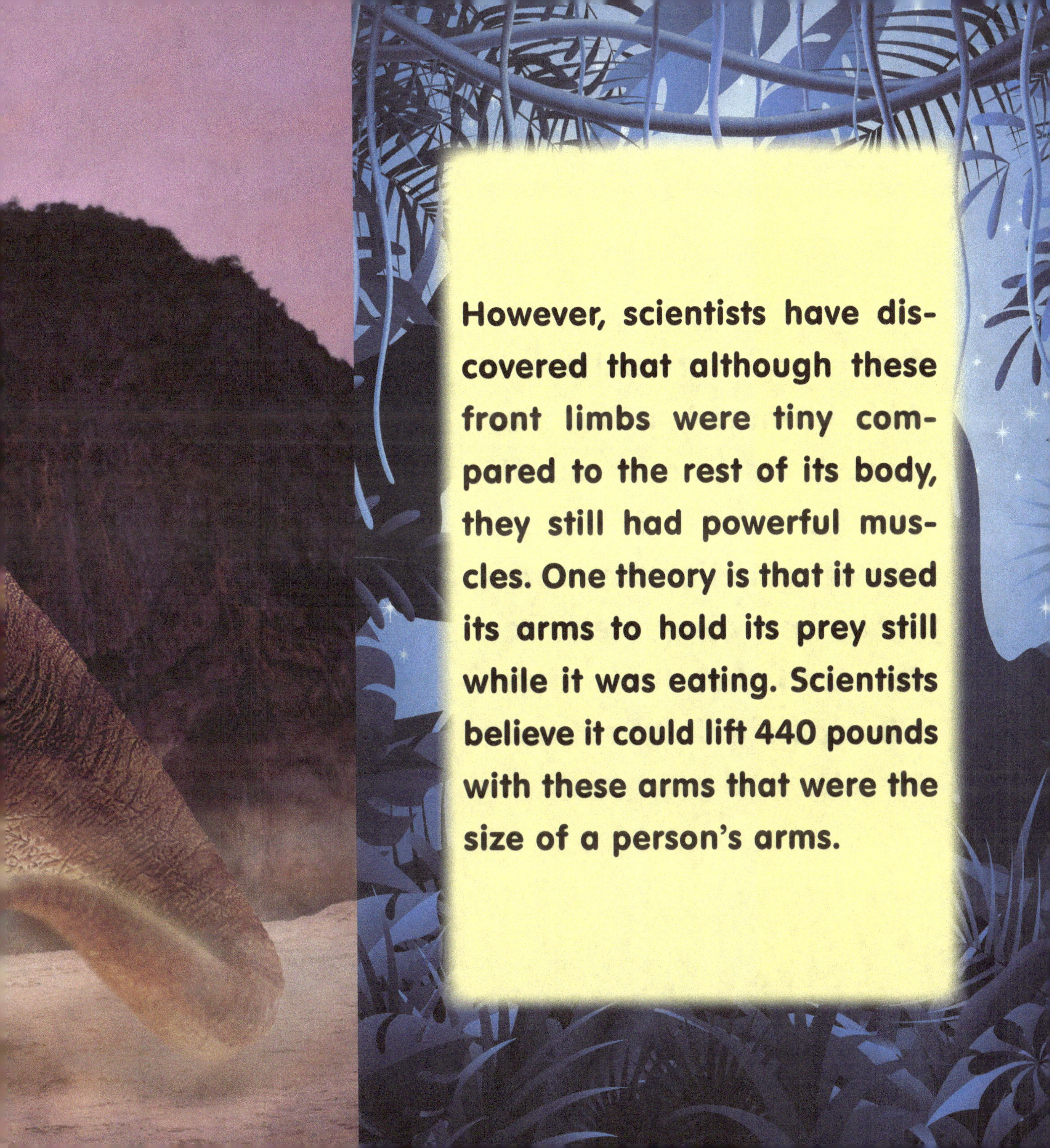

However, scientists have discovered that although these front limbs were tiny compared to the rest of its body, they still had powerful muscles. One theory is that it used its arms to hold its prey still while it was eating. Scientists believe it could lift 440 pounds with these arms that were the size of a person's arms.

Some scientists believe it held its mate in its arms or used them to push up off the ground if it fell. Many scientists believe the fore-limbs were completely use-less and that these huge dinosaurs didn't use them at all.

Dinosaurs actually have more in common with birds than reptiles do. If you've ever seen a chicken without its feathers you would see that that part of its skeleton looks just as strange as a T. rex's forelimbs.

The neck muscles of the T. rex are quite similar to the necks of modern birds. Birds use their heads and strong, flexible necks to hunt and eat. T. rex might have moved like powerful birds and killer whales eat. It would bite, then shake its jaws back and forth, and then twist off hunks of meat from its prey.

Recently, another much smaller dinosaur by the name of Gualicho shinyae was found in Argentina. It also has very tiny fore-limbs. Scientists are still searching for clues as to how T. rex used its tiny forelimbs or whether it used them at all.

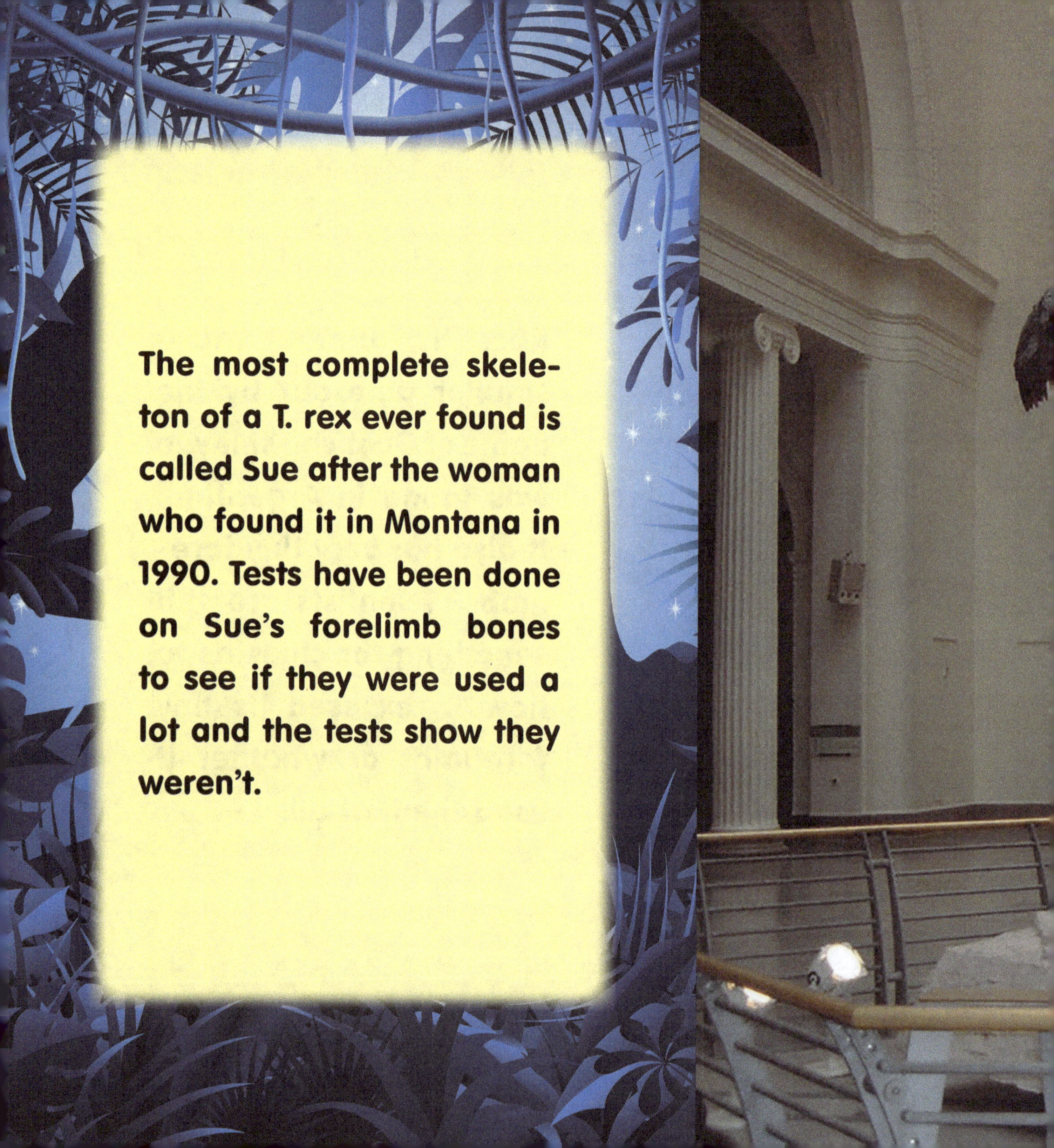

The most complete skeleton of a T. rex ever found is called Sue after the woman who found it in Montana in 1990. Tests have been done on Sue's forelimb bones to see if they were used a lot and the tests show they weren't.

Chicago Field
Museum

Tyrannosaurus Rex
named "Sue"

WHERE CAN I SEE THE SKELETON OF A TYRANNOSAURUS REX?

Sue is located in Chicago at the Natural History Museum. She was purchased for almost $8 million dollars.

In South Dakota, there is another excellent specimen at the Natural History Museum in Black Hills. That T. rex skeleton is called Stan. Barnum Brown found five different T. rex specimens and they are housed in New York at the Natural History Museum.

Museum of Natural History

WHAT DO WE STILL NEED TO LEARN ABOUT TYRANNOSAURUS REX?

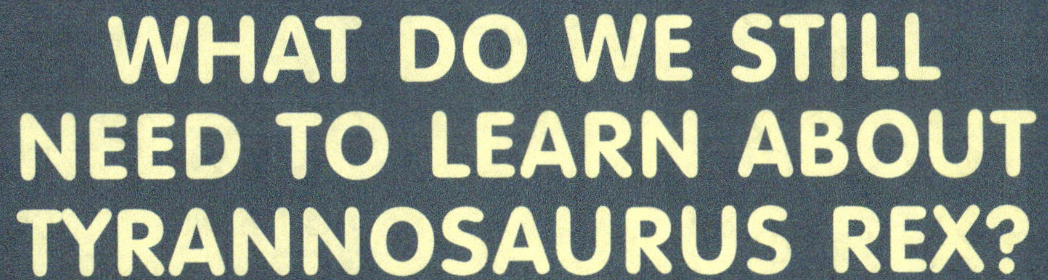

We can't tell what color skin the T. rex had because fossils don't give us that information. We don't know whether it had scales, feathers, or a combination of both. Despite the movies showing T. rex as a very fast runner, scientists are not absolutely sure if this gigantic dinosaur could run or not. If it couldn't run, then more than likely it was a scavenger.

For a long time, scientists thought that T. rex was the largest, meat-eating dinosaur. However in 1995, bones of what seemed to be a larger predator were found in the country of Argentina.

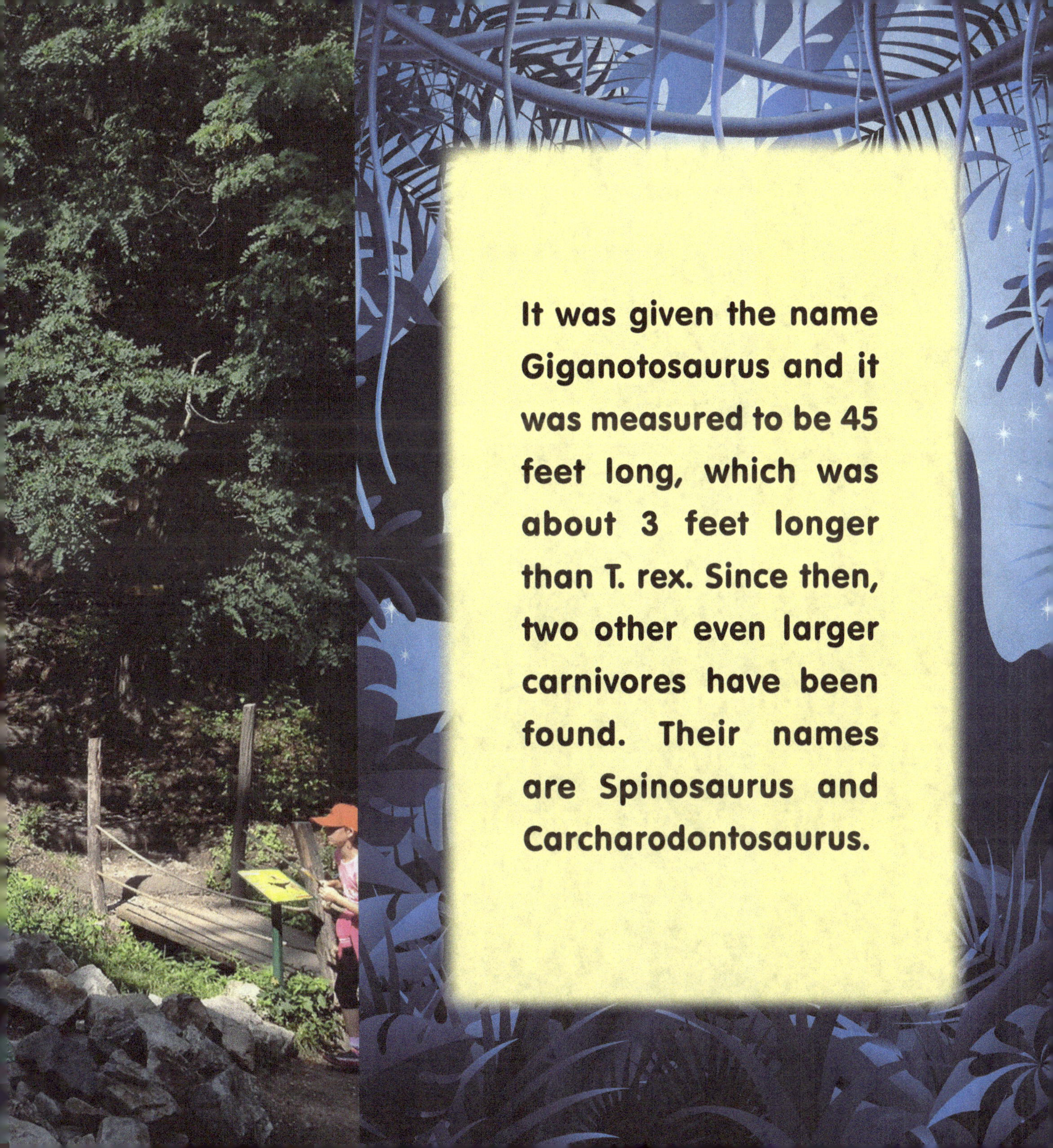

It was given the name Giganotosaurus and it was measured to be 45 feet long, which was about 3 feet longer than T. rex. Since then, two other even larger carnivores have been found. Their names are Spinosaurus and Carcharodontosaurus.

THREE FASCINATING FACTS ABOUT THE TYRANNOSAURUS REX

T. rex didn't have a way to brush its teeth so meat scraps would get lodged in its mouth. The bacteria would multiply so if the T. rex gave a bite to another dinosaur and didn't kill it, it would more than likely die days or weeks later from a bacterial infection.

Scientists aren't 100% sure of this, but there's a good chance that the female T. rex was heavier than the male by a few thousand pounds. Their hips may have needed to be bigger to carry T. rex size eggs! It's believed that a T. rex would have lived 30 years or more.

Awesome!

Now you know a lot more about the Tyrannosaurus rex. You can find more Animal books from Baby Professor by searching the website of your favorite book retailer.

Visit
BABY PROFESSOR
EDUCATION KIDS
www.BabyProfessorBooks.com
to download Free Baby Professor eBooks
and view our catalog of new and exciting
Children's Books

www.ingramcontent.com/pod-product-compliance
Lightning Source LLC
Chambersburg PA
CBHW080806120726
48001CB00009B/2867